BUM CANTOS, WINTER JAZZ, & THE COLLECTED DISCOGRAPHY OF MORNING

By
Rustin Larson

BLUE LIGHT PRESS ◆ 1ST WORLD PUBLISHING

1ˢᵗ WORLD
PUBLISHING

SAN FRANCISCO ◆ FAIRFIELD ◆ DELHI

WINNER OF THE **2013** BLUE LIGHT BOOK AWARD
BUM CANTOS, WINTER JAZZ, &
THE COLLECTED DISCOGRAPHY OF MORNING

1ST WORLD PUBLISHING
PO Box 2211
Fairfield, Iowa 52556
www.1stworldpublishing.com

BLUE LIGHT PRESS
www.bluelightpress.com
Email: bluelightpress@aol.com

AUTHOR PHOTO
Gaelen Watt

BOOK DESIGN
Melanie Gendron

COVER PHOTO
Rustin Larson

FIRST EDITION

LCCN: 2013912983

ISBN: 978-1-4218-8673-2

CONTENTS

ACKNOWLEDGMENTS

Some of these poems made their first appearance in print in the following magazines—

Illya's Honey (Bum Canto [Sitting on my bed, eyes closed,], Bum Canto [My uncle Slim, like a corpse.], Earth into Day, Floy Doy, Rummage)
Poets & Artists (The Machine, Tongue, Winter Jazz Up at the Group Home)
Future Cycle Poetry (My Father's Hernia)
The Bryant Literary Review (Photography)
Weather Eye (The Beetle, Mother & Son, Perfect)
Saranac Review (Anonymous, Oregon, Walking Alone)
California Quarterly (In League with Trees, Spider Conch—*Lambis Chiragra*)
Lilies and Cannonballs Review (Elegy)
Argestes (Damaged Enough, Electricity)
Natural Bridge (Night Troubles the Screen, Things the Photo Doesn't Tell)
Listenlight (Bum Canto [Meet me, she said.] {under the title Transformation and Sleep})
Midway Journal (Bum Canto [His life. His music.], Bum Canto [Transmogrify.])
Fact of the Universe: American Poetry Since Now (The Find)
The Mid-America Poetry Review (A Memory, My Lion, Shadows)
Poetry East (Bum Canto [Listening to] {under the title *Ach Der Lichter*}, Things I Tell My Children)
The Daily Palette (Great River Road, Winter)
North American Review (Attack the Ball)
MiPOesias (Andy Kaufman, Carroll Street)
Pirene's Fountain (The Collected Discography of Morning, *Il Ragazzo*, Life Documented)
The Potomac Review (Tar Roads)
GUD (Bum Canto [When he returned home from work,])
Diode (Bum Canto [Lassos of paint.], Bum Canto [I estimate by rule of thumb])—

and the author expresses his sincere gratitude to the editors—
many thanks also to Michael Carrino for his encouragement and attention to the words in this book.

To the memory of
Robert Long, Jack Myers, and W. E. Butts

Not "Revelation" —'tis—that waits,
But our unfurnished eyes—
—Emily Dickinson

BUM CANTO

When he returned home from work,
the day was just beginning.
Sleep, and memory sleeps
one hundred branches beyond.

He lugged the heavy frying pan up
from the cabinet and clanked it on the stove.
Winters: lawns turned monuments.
Admission's free.

The egg spread over the hot grease
like a map of the island.
Sleep, and my arms enclose mountains.
Sleep, and the world recovers

He sat on the sofa to eat. Part of the cushion
was chewed to ribbons. Was the dog losing
its mind. Sleep and be alone forever.
The vernacular? The America of Poets?

The headache didn't improve so he took
3 more aspirin and a shot of Scotch.
A microcosm of history?
Sleep, and someone feeds the tiger with his body.

It could be this way. A graveyard shift.
A basketball game on the TiVo.
My dad was William Blake.
I attended the University of Egg Salad (stanza break)

The crazy could open the door
and shoot the next student passing by
on scholarship. Roommate of Ezra Pound.
Sleep, and the thunder writes a poem

He will sleep naked and alone
lost in the filthy mouth of East St. Louis, Ill.
Great song in his heart, great song.
Hasn't sung it. But, by Jesus, he will.

RUMMAGE

for my mother

I ransack money from the dead, sell their
bowling balls and tap dance shoes. A loud rock
band parades itself down the block:
a tricked-out Camaro, two sub-woofers.

Our neighborhood drops another board or two—
the fences rot—drugs are dealt under the streetlight
near our mailbox. The storms have ceased to come through,
their moody bruise-purple hanging in the north.

There's the intersection where the gun battle took place—
the hostage, some lady we didn't know,
nailed by cop's bullets—they landed a
med-evac over there. You had to fly

to non-existence without your neighborhood—
without your Christmas twinkle-lights, your
can of snow-spray—without your good
fifty-pound box of recipes.

Maybe a snow will come this year, maybe the foot-
prints of a tiny child walking to school
with her backpack and lunch. The snow
with how many arms?

We emptied the house
of dad's tattered shirts,
your black bear of a winter coat,
the golf tees, the jewelry box with the silver certificate,

the Morgan dollar you thought would be
worth thousands by now. The table scarred by
the burning toaster: no more meals.
No more hash browns—

especially not near the window
and the way the sun came in to blind you,
breakfast over the steam of your coffee.
It blinded me, the place I sat after

your funeral. Dad would not speak to me
but lived in the silence of memory,
rooted the last of his disgust and tossed
it on the table with dirty radishes,

finally said to me because he could
not say it otherwise—though I looked
around the house and could only see
me as a child in illness near the few sources

of warmth there were—the squares of sun, the grate
of the furnace—supine, bronchitis-
prone, unwitting addict to the codeine
in Formula 44, constipated,

in various attitudes of discomfort and pain,
grimacing at the suppository rammed up my ass
by a caring finger—he said: she loved you;
you know that.

WALKING ALONE

Pavese was obsessed
with hills and women and night.

When tired, I find myself longing,
but not for this place.

A single-engine plane
low overhead; sun shining

on the leaves of the sycamore.
Pavese was obsessed

with wandering and returning.
We spend most of our lives returning.

This stone, eroded by sun and wind and rain,
will look like that woman, sentient

to a single curled, golden
leaf that rattles across

the gravel path. I could see it
even if I were blind.

Pavese was obsessed with hills
and rain.

He wrote one great poem
that really wasn't about the sea.

Today, I walk as far
as I can. Near some farm-

pasture, cows grazing. The land
undulates and curves in long loaves

of soil and grass. There is a pond
mid-distance, fringed by yarrow,

blazing stars.
Sometimes I think I can walk forever.

I skirt around
a tree and its huge roots,

imagine I am on a narrow
mountain pass, a bundle

of peacefulness and zero blame.
Back on the road, I nearly step on

and crush and kill
a tiny snake no longer

than a #2 pencil
and about as thick.

It immediately convulses
in a coil to strike.

I step over it,
and turn half-fondly to look,

but it keeps its poise
and rears back its head.

ANONYMOUS

So I'm thinking of my friend
for a few moments, that book of lean poems
he wrote. No one will ever know who he is.

He would always order rounds of Port at Julio's.
He would repeat the experience often.
Mr. whose name I can never

remember to spell with one or two t's.
It's a slushy day here.
It doesn't seem like a Port kind of day,

but for me it never is. Alcohol
doesn't mix well with the meds I'm on.
And no one will ever know who I am.

I will never learn the language of the angels
or translate their utterances
for the American Poetry Review.

I am stuck as you are, man—lodged
in the eye of the Cyclops
so all our other friends can escape.

I came to this library saying
to myself I'd write about my friend,
and lo and behold

there was a guy who looked just like you
keying himself into his Jeep
and driving off into the snow.

He had your funny cab-driver's
cap and his face was flushed,
for all I know, with Port.

He had a book in his hand
and a Styrofoam crate of medicine—
maybe hijacked flu vaccine.

If I didn't know you were still alive,
I would say he was your ghost.
The UPS truck comes up West Adams

as brown as the slush it rolls through.
Half the streets in this side of town
are named after presidents

who rest numbly beneath our soil
without a clue of what's become of us.
I write this to you because

this is just what it is. I used to have
a hat like yours. I bought it because
it was like yours. I wore it

because it was the color of Port
and I thought it would change
the way my head worked.

I wanted to look into the sky
and see your one-winged seagull.
Not far from here is the college

where I used to teach.
I'd teach whatever they told me to, man,
and I felt like an idiot.

I ached for the end of classes
so I could walk in the cold
and find my brain again.

I see some people still walking that way.
That's when I read your book,
and that's when I don't care

if anyone ever knows who we are.

BUM CANTO

His life. His music. His tomb of days and weeks.
He wore his father's circuitry; Franz felt deeply saddened;
he had tried so hard to please his father
in his head.

Today, no gulls jockeying above the river bend, no damaged Soviet
satellites, no collapsing orbit,
micro-antenna concealed in black eyeglasses.

But an eagle. Strength against the toothy planets, the rose bush
or sadness or light of the blue poplars,
and a red squirrel licks the snow under his car.

Unhappy in his work, transmitting thoughts of his unknown self
parallel the aroma of stale coffee, the dregs,
he filled his mind with music

and locked himself in his attic, a dim landscape, trembling green. Awaken
the body,
the cool stars mark the skin, burning August
creating one masterpiece after another.

He read Goethe and Barry Goldwater and the red enameled pin
awarding RCA serviceman of 1960. Then,
excitedly, soiled himself.

Rilke said, anticipating fall, brown and gold monarchs' flutter,
self-inflicted wounds being silent, the baby monster,
"I live my life in expanding obits."

Schubert said, unveiling the new synapses
withering, killing and resurrecting,

"Even a river gives itself the benefit of a doubt."

Iced over, the river still on a whim, soldering gun smoking, "O sacred heart,
my joy and inspiration . . ." he put to music
like
a disintegrator ray, at peace with what he had to do.
He had some options.
And later, "The Trout Quintet,"
famous the world over.

ELECTRICITY

drinking chai
Tuesday afternoon
February

the kids build a delicate Stonehenge
an ice cottage

water sings in the pipes in someone's kitchen
the thud of a dead man in the next apartment
Sarah is typing a letter

Anjalie moved to Hawaii
the sun breaks through a cloud
and the sofa is bathed in a rectangle of pale yellow

I move to look
I find the only real fiction is autobiography
knock knock knock

let me in says the ghost
the birds fly from bare tree-branch to branch
like the opening of a sonata

cardinals
red against the snow
I tell Sarah how to spell electricity

the curve of the branches
taken all together
suggests globes

especially later some nights
when they are glazed with ice
and filter the light of street lamps

this too
sonata I say
hearing the first few ghostly notes

WINTER JAZZ UP AT THE GROUP HOME

Patch of snow like an atoll, that was the last
question I had. Some grace before I knew
anything. There was a window in which
I bathed; not everyone can say that.
I had an interest in security; it's one of those
things. Before my images were because
of my readings of candle-flame. My scalp
like paper, this will get you nowhere.
It is just a waste, though important.
The truth-and-blood crew is reading in the garage.
The nurse will explain.

BUM CANTO

Lassos of paint. Lipped cigarette.
Autumn Rhythm. Lavender Mist. The season's
at our own end of reality; we take some tequila, lemon-salted,
Monday in Brooklyn, conversation lolling

self-destructive, semi-gloss; synapse patterns,
indescribable, the body and soul's conversation
like clouds over the river, stainless-steel light.
Pizza arrives with sausages that look like mitochondria.

Only he penetrated the emotional *cordon sanitaire*
he had thrown around his work-in-progress.
Centuries splash in wavelets. A shoe
falls like a dove from the bridge. Joanie shares a pint of milk.

Oedipus was a wreck. He needed three drinks
to nerve up to conversation, then the words drifted
with a cat she didn't know. Conversation takes
on a kind of ceramic quality. Almost bell-like.

Few, far between, mumbled phrases. It calmed him
to think, iron and brick and unsanitary
life staggering from a cab
with a letter from Karl we all just have to read.

TONGUE

The squid-tree waits for something to sail into its arms.

In daylight
the path is okay.

At night the place is thick with ghosts
and coyote tracks.

Right now it's a fairly average afternoon.
The waitress seems to know me,

the co-author of this new book
it's astonishing the Gestapo haven't disappeared.

In a totally dark room, do you see stars
where your hands should be?

We become acquainted with the spoons,
hope, overcast,

promise of thundershowers.
I hear children playing in the garden below,

half Hungarian,
half English on the tongue.

In a totally dark room,
do you see a foggy halo around a struck match?

The perimeter seems to talk to me.
Write something that means only to you.

In a totally dark room, do you hear the voice of a child?

SHADOWS

Summer. Grand Grandfather
and Great Grandmother Curin
sit on the running board
of their Model A.

Trees are full and it's Sunday
because there is the church
behind them. He has his pipe
in his right hand.

His overalls are his best and
clean—a thick blue shirt, crisp.
She wears a limp dress
with a pattern of the sky,

a swarm of lightning bugs,
pendant with the smoky red
luster of garnets. She is small,
heavy; he, thin, moustached

and smiling. On his right knee,
his grown daughter's shadow
appears: a photographer
with butterfly wings.

MOTHER & SON

Like Ginger Rogers twirling under the fat-faced and celestial spheres
you float by white irises
in your Easter dress

a couple pounds overweight
it's OK with me doll
the maple tree is new

the kids across the street
have slides
there is the boundary garden

the corn and tomato plants and green beans
your shoes are white
and standing on your shadow

which walks down into the earth
with a basket of pomegranates hooked on it's arm
the grass in need of trimming

noon
being washed by sun
in old neighborhoods

of butter and sugar and roughage
late May early September
I am me

throwing the yellow bandanna to ground
children on the twirling bars
at the school behind me

the grass worn
where father parks his truck at evening
the white travel trailer

gold zig-zag down the side
waits at Clear Lake
for the tornado

spine straight
a small boy with a neat haircut
and a life being built

THINGS THE PHOTO DOESN'T TELL

The places change. Did my grandmother cry
when she left her desert? Did my old man's
body crap out somewhere, fond of cigarettes
and salt peanuts? Everything had a funny flavor:
butter, victory. The boy holds the Boston terrier
in his arms like a baby. The dog is sleeping.
His sister comes home wearing her green-
and-yellow plaid uniform. Table and chairs
are those he remembers. Black legs, spic'n'
span linoleum. Grandmother stared out
the window with tears in her eyes and smashed
a whole stack of dishes with her hands.

MY FATHER'S HERNIA

I had a fruit salad for company
a bag of balloons, a sad monkey who wouldn't wake up

I am standing outside Utopia
in my tight army-green swim trunks

strangling a beach towel
the shadows of leaves brushing the clapboards

I have many deposits
of fat on my back and chest though I will tell you it's pure muscle

I sacrificed my groin in some accident in the navy
or in Chicago lifting a washer up 12 flights of stairs

my legs are familiar white hairless
you'll recognize them as your own when you're 44

I have no neck, I have an appetite
I'm still celebrating the end of the war

the grass is soft here
we'll go to the sailors' emporium for fried clams

and ride the empress after sunset
or maybe the queen or the chief

ride on the bumper cars roller coaster hammer of death
and listen to the Twins play on the radio

in the dark and listen to the lake water still itself
until the light morning breezes something illegible

a matter of myself, the dock spelling itself
plank by plank out over the water

DAMAGED ENOUGH

I still my heart and I can hear you,
the laughter they have in the sun.

I picture the raft rolling on the waves a speedboat made.
I hear you on your trampoline near your garden

with the water off and all the transparency in place
to cue the world for the next instance of now.

This was all there was to importance, I suspect.
You are petting the black kitty

though she is so wary,
you in your striped shirt,

holding up the dead squirrel for show.
The world is not damaged enough,

though your mother sighs as she says
what's it all coming to,

going to the dogs
as a mottled stray yelps down the street

chased by the future suicide's hotrod 55 Chevy
with the chrome header and fat rear tires.

Your door slams directly below,
and I know exactly where the past is now

as your mother fries up the taco shells
and sprinkles salt on the daikon radishes.

I am forever sun-warm cement, and you
are spraying water from a hose.

The sun will soon end the day,
but we are not through with it yet.

There is another light to match,
another scarecrow to burn in the human tree.

FLOY DOY

Fats Waller gleaming in a light as green as money,
and we walk in the East Village,

a woman sprawled out on the steps
and moaning like she is making love to Jesus Christ,

and I ask if maybe she needs an ambulance or something.
Just one more day trader slumming

the weekend away on blotter
in search of a vision as Wordsworth might have said,

or was it Coleridge,
I don't know.

There are Jamaicans selling ganja incense
and Walt Whitman who says you can suck his if you want to.

We had Chinese earlier,
fortunes read.

I lift a photo from the memory box.
There we are in the booth, and I have eyes that glitter

like a rodent;
you want France in your pants;

the next frame shows blue-eyed Ricky with his cowboy gun.
We all wanted to protect ourselves.

I swear we heard giants pounding down the boulevard
with great thorny baseball bats for a living.

I visited a stranger's grave for you and left flowers
and had a weird stretch of luck.

Now I am writing this to you wherever you are:
New York, Massachusetts in the rain,

at Concord on your one-gear bicycle.
It is right it is wrong it is right it is wrong.

I spelled forward time backwards in bones
and it worked out for me.

A sweater, a fire.
The woman was really making it with Christ.

Waller sang years after he had died under a cathedral
of sodium lamps.

BUM CANTO

Transmogrify. The change from your pocket. Cold,
I was driving a Studebaker. Huge sexual flowers.
Crusts of cheese. Gas gauge: life sputtered

silver dust. Driving alone. True atheist. Escaped
from a pan of simmering milk, our bedtime drink.
Clarified butter and honey, the yellow of pregnancy

fell into books, David Copperfield, school-boy's agony
drowned smelling the milk of the moon and Detroit,
"You are a handsome death," I said,

drawing skeletons on the inside cover. Exhausted stare.
Who stood on the bridge in Detroit
dreaming of Windsor, Ontario?

The vacuum of morning, softly gathering flurries;
if my fingers were darts, I would have won every game.
That diner will be dust someday. *El diablo de la escuela frio.*

The bleached stalk of milkweed, interplanetary blackness
inches from Big Chief Kiss-My-Tuchas's
teepee lodge and snake-oil ambrosia stand.

College town, 1980. To describe this, you dropped
the subject altogether, carrot stick, the glow of milk,
and the petrified forest sang. 7-Up bottle in the Men's Room.
The big parrot in the dining room squawked.

Cafeteria drowned, December 14th. Window's fine
snow crystals, north wind, justified lines, flannel shirt,
my heart felt ecstatic as a shotgun wound.
I plunged my hand through the lunch counter,

cool as the coffee sang upstairs, smell of oil,
and the stickshift of the Studebaker mumbled,
"Home at last."

THE MACHINE

The man sucked into the machine, the machine
becomes another tool like a ball-point pen
and his blood ink. He writes with his
body and his death, and he makes the news-
paper, name withheld until notification.

Don't try to make good on something bad
the mother tells the child and the child ain't
listening. The movie seems like a lake
into which he can pool himself, starlight
and cigarette, and swim, swim toward the beacon and panic.

He started to panic in the middle of the lake,
he reported, and he got cramps and started
to go under if it weren't for Mark's cigarette
glowing on the shore there with his dog Valiant.

This was just another example of the machine.
I guess I had no idea that it would affect
me in the motel room. I hung my towel
on the idea rack and flicked on the television,
my life playing in re-run again and the
nasty Vermont earth and Rolling Rock.

The child grew up and became a successful
human being. The machine ran well ignorant
of its true purpose until that day came,
I would like to say again, though it is the
same point in time without beginning middle
or end. Someone had to nonetheless
clean up the man's urgent message.

BUM CANTO

Sitting on my bed, eyes closed,
drilling the core of my extreme
Hindu prayer, my roomie
at his desk, practicing dialogue,

beer, fox grapes, the window, tendrils gripping screen mesh,
little hands, spider-gauze, cold and merciless thoughts:

"He screamed and
screamed and screamed
and screamed . . ."

Breathless winter hands. Mid-term exams. Panic in the hallway
of the library, looking for something greater than memory
or the nectar of revision,
his blood.
My eyes open,
glimpse his smile:

red and white half-pint milk cartons and soggy paper
straws. Doobie. More beer. The microfiche file. Under tables with the lint

trying to get it
just so: "Have a mint? They're
imported from Germany!"
A cowboy

and pencil butts, a small twang in the heart, a piece
of ice on the Pennsylvania Turnpike, blue, shaped like

a clown, balancing on his hands
mid-novel, mints spilling from
his shirt pocket as he tries again:
"Here's a mint, have one, they're

West Virginia, like that folk instrument called the sweet
potato. Thirst translates itself into mountains, the handiwork

imported." That's enough,
"imported."
Light blue, floating, clouds

of a dentist's drill, what a good body does in the face
of his own extinction, before any certainty or blizzard

or fantastic sunburst of Bach:
"Have a mint,
they're German."
Then the Wallendas mess up

through an invasion of hashish smoke, ambiguous yellow
pills, leafy faces against the window, hungry, devouring

the high wire and falling,
no net:
"He screamed and screamed," he says.
"He screams and he screams,"

in a moment of ice, shots, gleaming wind, Pennsylvania.

IL RAGAZZO

Ragazzo, ragazzo where are you?

Are you in the *campi* with the *cavallo*?
Are you barefoot, shirtless; do you

think you are a thousand Indians
charging over the suntanned hill,

sticks of thunder brandished
in your fist, the encampments

below you drowsy with smoke
and breakfast? *Ragazzo,*

lungs, legs wondering
on the edge of drowning;

come back to me guitars in firelight.
Oh, marshmallow of the moon,

river of off-brand cola, near the Triple-
"A" ballpark, July with fist in fat

leather, a program screaming Vida
Blue. *Il ragazzo* climbs under the bleachers

for dropped quarters among
the peanut shells, drizzle of Grain Belt,

lazy clapping of women trolling
for their evening's work,

sustenance, and tomorrow's eggs
at the Holiday Inn. *Il ragazzo*

does nothing but go about
his grimy business, takes the unlit

roads home in the fish-
dark, lights a birthday candle

to his battered mattress,
his loft of nightmares, broken hockey

sticks. *Il ragazzo* smokes a stolen cigarette,
ponders dropping out
of the sky.

ATTACK THE BALL

My father says, pitching it to my glove,
"Don't let it attack you."
I taste the leather, pound my fist
In the pocket, feel the crack
Of the planet hitting my palm.
Attack the ball, kick the earth,
Invent the soil, sweat and let
The trees applaud in a gust,
Throw the spinning world we must
Toward each other, father and son,
While neighbors lacquer their hot rod
The color of mid-autumn
And the fumes make us high. Attack
The ball, catch a bomb, launch a missile,
Throw for home with the eyes of raccoons
In the burdock, and eyes of sparrows
In the elms, branches rotting and falling,
Twigs we call first,
Second, and third, utility pole we call
Foul, gopher dust and the smoky breeze
With October flaming in the trees.

A MEMORY

I remember a bird high
above the spire, a goiter
full of fish, it would fly
inland a bit and reconnoiter
a likely place, far from bicycles
and angelic lads who'd loiter
with sticks as sharp as icicles
near the nesting grounds. It would reach
its place, if half-diseased
in feather, an idyllic "beach"
rimmed with tires and freshly deceased
creatures of the sea.

BUM CANTO

Meet me, she said. A kiss. Light of a gold coin.
That's the body's death. Let all the past be there.
The past glitters like clothes of a hovering angel,
a fairy tale, window's well: oxygen and citron. Light
of night. He'd found a song worshipping
an almost remembered play. These are my words.
He had been writing along smooth plaster walls. She holds
this for ages, holding the words, walking past the houses.
Life was a crumpled letter, hair bound in a braid,
a raw overwhelming landscape, but for a cascade.
I didn't intend the gardens you see as you walk, the darkness
you wrap, curls that pour near your ears to a froth
of lace. Oranges on a hill near. Sparrows. Grow
yourself from air. Play on parched grass, simple cart path
paraded by blue flags, honey bees. On her bed,
mean it; it finds breath committed in a bowl of apples
and apricots spilled, a Persian throw of blue and red,
where you see her, 5 a.m., the traffic glowing like a false dawn.
I did. Metal insects sliding into song.
You hear the notes of stars playing the lawns.
Shake the globe. It's starlight crumbled to a powder, fallen to earth.
The night I was dying, night of the population,
*some*one's soul was torn in two—the silver snow
of forgetfulness sparkled in the room.
The night she (one's self back from a seed)
was born, I lay dead. You don't need
rainfall on transcendental soil. No, let the soil
light around you. The starlight became my cloak.

EARTH INTO DAY

I cook meals at this little place, same five customers
every evening. It overlooks the tennis courts,
and sometimes two beefy girls swat a ball across the net
until some of the lower stars weep. Generally,
I amaze my diners with the many variations
of fowl with sauce I concoct, each dish served
with a refreshing dry white. Now though, the kitchen
cleared and the pans drying on their racks, I sit
in my room and listen for the few passersby
on the darkened courts, the smell of rose incense drifting
from someplace. The girl squeals and I know
she is with that same fellow, walking to the park
and the trails through the oak trees. Their voices
grow fainter as they walk—their
silhouettes against cold April.
If I close my eyes, I can almost hear
the edge of the world scraping against some distant light,
some change of earth into day, where markets
are opening and vegetables and flowers light the roads
with their colors. I don't know if I'll ever go there.
I play a few chords on my guitar, then sip some wine,
then recline my head on a stack of three pillows
and wait for sleep to overtake me.

GREAT RIVER ROAD

Sunday morning, a place
in a little gravel town—long road like a ribbon
marking the ravine of gospel—
some toast and coffee in a lack of concern,
meat market on one side, television shop
on the other, a smattering of houses—families
weird-bred, stinking of unwashed clothes
and a stream of starlings in the mulberries
hedging the railroad's diagonal cut into the hot zone
of heaven's brain.
Driver pulls beside a row of lamp post wreaths,
leaves the sucker running as he sits
at the counter, puddles lighting the sky
blue, a tall stack, hash-browns. I slept there
many days with a pad of paper under my head,
Nutcracker suite playing, some kid banging
out 100,000 on pinball. I was becoming
a cup half full, the coffee maker thumping maniacally;
the waitress slid the fabric of her hip
against my shoulder.
3-cheese omelet, quarter playing Merle Haggard,
the short-order dwarf sweated in his cage of steam.
Cash register rang its miracles to the floor.
Marijuana withered tall behind the propane tank.
A coward rose to confront the sun and keep running away.
Swallows swung overhead. I drank my consciousness
to the horizon. The sun grew round and red.

LIFE DOCUMENTED

but not the life lived. Near exhaustion, but
what have I done? On a whim, I take a shovel
to the yard and dig. Neighbors splay their blinds to watch me.
What is down there? I find coins and a bunch of bones.
I find an old telephone and an iron and a hit pipe some
teenager must have chucked in a panic. I find old blue
and brown medicine bottles, a cameo ring of a girl
with a garland in her hair. There are large rusted needles
and nails and hinges from cabinets.
There are porcelain knobs and shards of crockery.
There is the barrel and cylinder of an old pistol—
knife blades and tarnished silver spoons.
I dig until the moonlight fails me and I can see nothing
forever. Then I sit down on the edge
of what I am and let the wind sing in my mouth.

BUM CANTO

I estimate by rule of thumb,
celebration of the opened heart.
Woman clutching her throat,
the buzzard circling comfortably.
Charismatic, I'm here. And I'm there.
Paradiso. Just another thing
a quarter mile off has what
it needs now. I won't go to work with it. I was quite sure
once. Now I've lost the point,
roaming out into alleyways;
there is only and this where she should walk
in the room and say,
but she doesn't and I don't.
I think, perhaps, this began
as indictment; the bear-
claws are suspect; the most
penetrating question comes
from an ATM; you
can't imagine thirty years ago as I sat in my
parents' house with my copy
of *The Portable Faulkner*
why anyone
lives here. Meanwhile,
at the tire store, the gumballs
harden in their machine;
the fan turning my lamp lights my book.
The crickets had built a huge
song toward the sky. I realize
on the ceiling down to the fools on TV
playing ball. Words in a notebook
become more fascinating,
and, at last, how I got here. I think I'm

snapping out of it, and I'm
grateful for all those things.
Who cares?
That small rodent
of a heart leaps out of your left
breast pocket and makes
a break for it, right into
the lunch-hour traffic outside
Hy-Vee. Little feller never
had a chance. You could go
to the hospital; more on that later. Faulkner's
voice. My dad making a summer
sausage sandwich and settling,
but they wouldn't
know what's wrong with you.
You might. They got me here. Here is OK.
Fantastically, it is the same sun
that saw me into this world—
weird, unhinged—
as well, take that
vague sense of confusion.
Wash it on delicate and
dry it the same and wear it
because it's the only thing
that matches.

OREGON

in memory of Robert Long

My friend says
most poems are bad.
He has stopped liking poetry,
lives on Long Island these days
with a mile of infection;
I know where he is.
Once, when I was ill, I lay
dreaming this sick feeling
was a road, a highway
actually, through the mountains.
There were signs
posted for rock fall.
When I started to feel better,
the ocean was in sight—
Gold Beach, Oregon, in fact—I stood
and strolled with my jacket zipped tight
and threw pieces of driftwood
at the waves. There was a moment
I found some money in the sand—
assorted coins—amounting to about
$3.86. Quite a find
when you think about it.
I can't remember what I did
with the money—
bought a sandwich no doubt.
Anyway, it felt good
to be in Oregon.

PHOTOGRAPHY

Earth takes a long-exposure photo of herself—
her apartment a kind of camera obscura—
the image of snowflakes burned on the wall—

She sits opaque in this light—
the messages come
steadily from across the sea:

Puffer fish died young in the afternoon,
winter light, months before the migration
and the cherry blossoms. Oh, wandering field

of grass, you are the only thing left
of the warrior's ambition. You were what
the light had to offer: The day photographed,

imperfect, stuttering,
in marginal health and state of mind, the sound
of clocks slicing off bits of time.

BUM CANTO

Listening to
German opera,
I hear a series
of doors slamming

above me.
Then I remember.
There is no floor
above me.

THINGS I TELL MY CHILDREN

There is a giant eyeball living
under the staircase.
There is a giant eyeball
and seven dancing devils.

Yes, I can make you a bird suit
so you can teach yourself to fly.

Never forget you are an alien life form.

Some years ago my father dug himself out of his grave,
tooled around town
in a yellow '75 Impala.

It came in handy now and then.

So if in the future
you're at your rope's end,
don't hesitate
to call. I will dig
myself upward, reconstitute
my ashes, press my scattered
voices together with the glue
of ether, stand by your shoulder
like a whirlwind.

WAITING FOR EVENING TO COME

As I wait for evening to come,
clouds drift: fish-shaped loaves of bread.
People walk home from their meditations.

Under my window,
a teenage boy carries garbage; a man in a green jacket
whistles, "Won't You Be My Baby Bumble-Bee?"

At a rabbit
a Chinese toddler points her finger;
the northern magnolia sheds its last blooms.

Like a litter of newborn muskrats
in a pile on the floor, my socks.
Oh, where will we walk this evening?

BUM CANTO

My uncle Slim, like a corpse.
It gets so late you confuse the clock

inside his sheet at the nursing home
with a pan of tuna casserole.

He could move; he didn't want to.
Dead for years. Some guru plays,

when he hears his brother's voice,
sitar on the radio. The police

stare. Slim's face
hasn't howled for hours. You,

a hard pudding of flesh,
wonder where you got this big scab,

whiskers. That's what it's like to stand,
to vaguely remember a baby rattlesnake

before a man who wants to feel,
dangling as you walked past the water,

nothing. All of baseball
is a treatment plant. Black squirrel

was history. There was a picture,
jauntily perched on a pine knob,

of Jesus before a television.
How long the squirrel's tail was as he groomed

my red-eyed alcoholic cousins.
Sleep won't come as they lead their lives of work

toward this place, cold sheets,
stare at a bamboo flute, the coffee table, cold rooms, no where to go,

only one thing to wait for.

IN LEAGUE WITH TREES

Giant Coast Redwood. Not here,
of course. Out there at the edge
of the continent, singing to the ocean.
One rose hung upside-down,
dried to a crisp. A sink of dirty
dishes. A book of love poems,
but not the kind of love poems
you'd expect. Wind chilling
the house, good cold singing wind.

ELEGY

I would speak to the disembodied spirit of
composition that its mist-like fingers
move the stylus of the Ouija board
of my headache and revive
the mummified lips of pedagogy
never mind reading these
never mind the highway is long
never mind the turns through the orchard hills
the muted autumn
and the script of water
it is now ours to hold
the orange smoke of leaves
the lavender haze across the dry cornfields
the sonnets of kitchen gardens
the sestinas of highway signage
lonely in the child of
my self warm wrapped in the arms
of being lost troubled in the
omnipresence I feel I say not
quite understanding inarticulate
unprepared doomed but just one
of the brothers traveling
traveling

THE BEETLE

Yesterday, walking on the outskirts of some forest
with my three daughters, we came upon
a brilliant green beetle recently loosed
from earth's jewel box. Skirting up
an embankment of well-trod mud, the beetle
shone brightly as the sun touched its shell.
Soon Sarah kicked off her shoes
and headed for the muddy trickle
through the woods. I want to walk
up this stream, she said, and looked
over her shoulder. How far will you
walk with me, she said, How far?

PERFECT

The perfect cat makes you happy. The radiator
crisping the ferns makes you happy. The white
wine makes you dizzy and hyper and panicked
and then happy. The fact that this moment will
always be in 1974, Iowa City, makes you happy.
Since you have a sore throat that will develop
into bronchitis and leave you weak with a quilt
around your shoulders as you lean over the table,
shivering, drinking Nort's bouillon cubes,
that makes you happy. That the guest-
room with its ugly linoleum and pissy mattress
looks so angry for your sake, makes you happy.
Because the west at the end of December
(at this hour) is a wine staining everything, you
are happy. But nothing will last forever,
and the years will peel away from the wall with a touch.

SPIDER CONCH—LAMBIS CHIRAGRA

That cold November, we walked down the length
of our beach, climbed the switchback staircase
up the tide wall to "Thistle," our rental. Water,

a bucket of clams, a fire, tide-rise
was pulled in by the moon's bone body.
We dreamt in the coast's darkened horns.

The conch was left on our doorstep, its horns
a strange compass in daylight, its thorny length
equal to my hand which held its body

like a weapon. I spied down the staircase
to see who left it, who might, walking, rise
in the distance, footsteps erased by water.

There was no one. You put on the water
for coffee, the steady blue flames like horns
lifting the kettle. I felt your curiosity rise

when I showed it to you, placed it on the length
of the table. You disappeared up the staircase
for your camera, then had me pose with its body

crabbed over my heart; I acted out a body
in anguish. Click. This is how memory works. Water
was busy with its breaking. The beach, the staircase

to the sea, was as smooth as sleep. The devil's horns
on my forehead were lovely, you said. Length
of love, your hands in my pockets. Sunrise.

I took the spider conch to a rise
of sand and placed it there; my body
bowed in supplication. You laughed. Down the length

of the beach, gulls cried; the foaming water
fizzed its bitter ale; the six horns
of the conch pointed to the horizon.

THE FIND

Everything I've found
continues to find itself
wherever it is hidden.

Someday I will split
an apple—and there—
complete—whatever it is.

I could have chosen nothing,
but I have chosen struggle.
It pays about the same.

MY LION

My lion watches from the kitchen window
and listens to the schoolboys yelling *hai-YA*!

He breathes his loud purrs and then roars,
grunts rhythmically
as the afternoon drains into gutters.

He would like to prowl and prance
the savanna free and eat a villager,
and I would like nothing better
than to unlock the door and hold it open.

My lion pads up to my recliner, licks my feet.

The Hungarians downstairs are afraid
of his sheer weight and power everyday
pounding above them.

He claws up to my shoulders
and gives my neck a playful bite.
I know (and he knows) he could snap me, like that!

This is what keeps us so close.

ANDY KAUFMAN

He came to
wrestle the girls, and he
found one that he liked
with frizzy black hair and
huge knockers, and he
said, "I'm takin' her home
to momma," and we were
all in the cafeteria then,
and we were students, and
we were in a circle around
the guy who played conga
drums on Saturday Night
TV, and we were smiling
and laughing and pressing
around trying to get a
better look, and I think
the circle tightened some
and Andy got this
wide-eyed look
and his face went pale
like he thought suddenly
we were all going to
kick the shit out of him or
eat his brain.
But then his friend
or whatever
stepped up and

said, "Come on, guys. Give
Andy some room." So we
backed off and slowly
scattered, a little sorry
we had panicked him,
but maybe thinking this was
just part of the performance
anyways.

CARROLL STREET

Fall turns parchment; there's something you'd write
upon each leaf held under a slanted evening light.

In her seminar on Cervantes you wrote, "Miguel de Unomuno."
Some mad Hungarian whistled an unnerving vibrato

in the garden. You do what you do. She's dead, yet the brain says,
"I wonder what she is doing now." In the afterlife, they're just settling

into cigarettes and coffee and better conversation.
Julia left out milk and fruit last night for the departed.

It is a cool on/off raining day today, the day I always imagined
I'd make a million and enjoy a brandy and cigar at The Club.

You believe there is a train that goes there.
Upon the platform, carrying something in your hand. It is unclear.

I always dreamed I was a boy in 1919 in a fruit market. I read Yeats'
    "All Souls' Night."
When William Blake died, witnesses say the room filled with a golden
    light.

Leaving implies destination. The wind has blown most of the leaves
    from the sycamore.
On the Metro, the train stalled on a trestled ramp near

Rhode Island Avenue, everyone crammed in. The after-work crowd, dead
from a day in the government: breathless as the train stuck.

The aroma of sage fills the house.
You put on your coat and walk out into the cool air

for a while. I don't know what most thought—
what would it be like, five hours, six, standing, holding

onto a bar of polished steel, watching the city as night fell,
listening to the moans and the sighs of the hungry?

You see the withered garden, the gray-blue-mottled sky,
the black squirrel gnawing on something you are sure is an eye.

But the train slipped back a couple notches to some shouts,
and then it lurched forward and we were on our way.

You see twigs you think are the hand of death, see money
blowing across the soccer field, run after it. It turns out to be nothing.

Silver Spring in twilight. We left the train and walked to the rooms
we had rented. "This is Dante and you are sleeping," she once said.

These perhaps are lessons. Tenuous. That's the word.
At this age now, not a comforting one, but no big deal.

But even now there's a part of you convinced they're all permanent and
   real.

WINTER

We live at the bottom of a sea of snowflakes.
They fall ruled by a mathematics
no one can resolve. When my brother

reads my poems, his brain turns to mineral.
The dawn's yarn
knits itself into an evening sky. (Flowers are snowflakes

grown wise.)
If I empty the wallet of my memory, evoke the mathematics
of emotion, scrape the excess mineral

of my loyalty, I can recognize my brother
as he was, soldering the radio together. The smoke, the mineral
encrusting the hot iron, the pure snow

of radio static, "Woolly Bully." Brotherhood
of sparrows, mathematics
of prayer, accumulation of snowflakes

sloping against the basement window,
night walks like a brother
up from the bus stop and pauses in an urn

of lamplight on the sidewalk to smoke.
It's the winter we learn to breathe mineral;
every breath is a breath earned;

confident I'll see somehow another summer;
not certain whether I'll see this brother
again this or any other season.

TAR ROADS

August dusk and heat of day would still be
there. A bare foot would sink its shape
in a soft patch, and sometimes the patch would ooze
an eye of purest black. Tar did not
come off sweetly in the bath. Sometimes it was
the badge of summer worn well into autumn
and not erased but by the friction of a winter's
worth of socks and sorties up the sledding hill
and down into the skidding brake of snow.
On the iced streets there was still tar below.

THE COLLECTED DISCOGRAPHY OF MORNING

I went on a trip when I was 16.
Concrete boiled in ballets of paisley;
trees coiled and uncoiled, writhing, it seemed,

in ecstasy. She said I was merely seeing
time itself accelerated. I never questioned this.
A cold day I will walk

around the courthouse, admire the resin-cast
replica of Liberty, smile as people leave
the Lutheran church for their meals of shadow.

I will think
how it was years ago,
think around the rain-tight skin,

the clothes that spoke, the jeans
that fit, drum-tight, the purse of mandalas,
incantations, the money

like lost wings.
I will play the collected discography of morning,
the rain, the house carved from bone.

NIGHT TROUBLES THE SCREEN

Darkness had a bicycle, tapping, flowing
through a city—come hither.
If the drone of the fan (it was morning)
were music (and I thought you were a snow

of petals), it would say endlessness.
It was evening. The only things are moments.
Standing on the frontier of an enchanted forest,
I thought you were ribbons of orange water.

Birds became friends. Lightning flashed.
The rain fell in sheets poured from up; the air
flowed behind you. I walked the infinite stretch
of concrete to school like a scarf, again,

wrapped in yellow. I followed the forest path
to the middle of SILK, my daydream.
There was a cottage. Everything was lit,
but there was no music. I tried the door handle.

The curtains were pale, glowing white.
I could hear sparrows gossiping in the eaves.
(Even now, though night engulfs, small bits
of ice are raining on the roof like sand pelting,

sliding down the gray slabs of shale. There
is a flickering light in the window.) I thought
about you, I usually do, but I also thought
about the silent ones I had dreamed of,

and how it is always raining in some fashion
when I awake. The door handle (I had
my books and papers strewn near my bed
on the floor) was as warm (you were so
far away from me) as a woman's hand.

ABOUT THE AUTHOR

Rustin Larson's poetry has appeared in *The New Yorker*, *The Iowa Review*, *North American Review*, *Poetry East*, *Saranac Review*, *Poets & Artists* and other magazines. He is the author of *The Wine-Dark House* (Blue Light Press, 2009) and *Crazy Star* (selected for the Loess Hills Book's Poetry Series in 2005). Larson won 1st Editor's Prize from *Rhino Magazine* in 2000 and has won prizes for his poetry from The National Poet Hunt and The Chester H. Jones Foundation among others. A seven-time Pushcart nominee, and graduate of the Vermont College MFA in Writing, Larson was an Iowa Poet at The Des Moines National Poetry Festival in 2002 & 2004, a featured writer in the DMACC Celebration of the Literary Arts in 2007 & 2008, and he was a featured poet at the Poetry at Round Top Festival in May 2012.

Printed in the United States of America

.

www.ingramcontent.com/pod-product-compliance
Lightning Source LLC
Chambersburg PA
CBHW032029090426
42741CB00006B/785